This book is dedicated to my fourth born child and only daughter, Carlena Joanne. She is the perfect combination of both parents and has brought so much joy into our lives.

A Close Up Look at

Theodore Roosevelt

National Park

By Josie Zayac

Theodore Roosevelt National Park, home to bison, elk, and deer. They're wonderful to look at, but don't get too near!

Take a close look.
What have we here?

stove for cooking

writing desk

(Theodore Roosevelt wrote more books than any President)

It is the cabin of a hunter, containing all his gear.

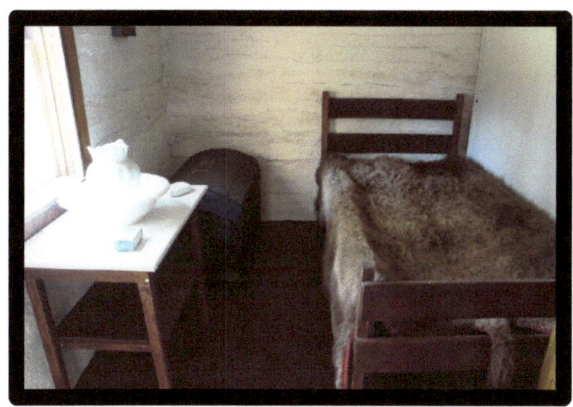

trunk, bed, and wash stand

stove for heat

Take a close look.
What do you see?

Prairie coneflowers . . .

. . . and yellow sweet clover.

So many flowers- growing all over!

Take a close look.
What do you see?

It may be a weed, but I think
it's pretty.

Take a
close
look.
What
do you
see?

Echinacea looks like a
badminton birdie.

Take a close look.
What do you know?

It's silver sage. On the path it did grow.

Take a close look.
What do you see?

Buffalo berry used to make
relish and jelly.

Take a close look.
What do you see?

It's petrified wood that once
was a tree.

Take a close look.
What do you see?

Inside a cave is too dark
 for me.

Take a close look.
What do you see?

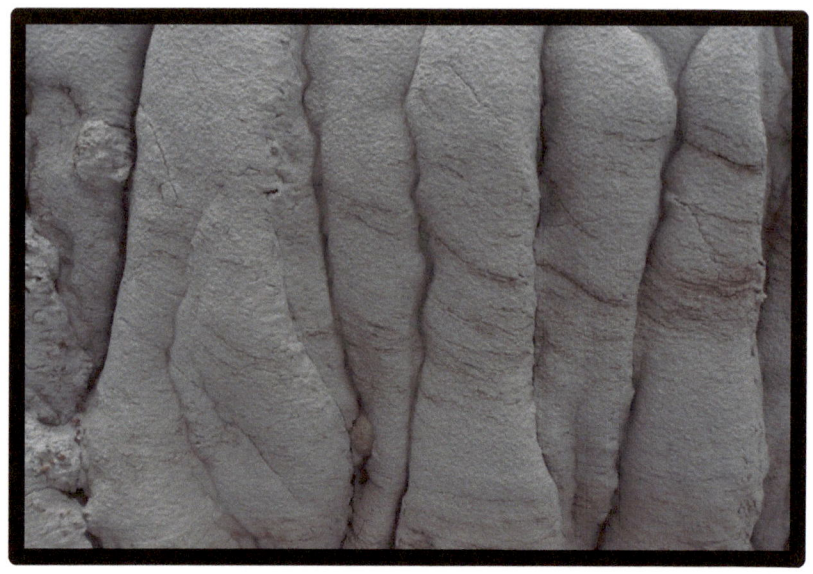

It looks like an elephant foot to me.

Take a close look.
What do you see?

It's a cactus. Don't touch-
it's prickly.

Take a close look.
What do you see?

It's a big old buffalo.
Don't come towards me!

Buffalo, also called bison, were once almost extinct. But now they are protected. That's a good thing, don't you think?

Take a close look
at everything around.
So many interesting sights
abound.

From geological formations
to flowers and game.
Once you look at nature,
You never feel the same.

Facts about Theodore Roosevelt National Park, North Dakota

- The first and only National Memorial Park
- Established by President Truman on April 25, 1947
- On November 10, 1978 the name changed to Theodore Roosevelt National Park
- 100 square miles in size
- It is the only National Park in North Dakota
- Park contains 3 areas of badlands
- Cover picture is Theodore Roosevelt's cabin

Look for other National Park books by Dr. Josie Zayac

- A Close Up Look at Bryce Canyon National Park
- A Close Up Look at Crater Lake National Park
- A Close Up Look at Cuyahoga Valley National Park
- A Close Up Look at Joshua Tree National Park
- A Close Up Look at Redwood National and State Parks
- A Close Up Look at Rocky Mountain National Park
- A Close Up Look at Sequoia National Park
- A Close Up Look at Theodore Roosevelt National Park
- A Close Up Look at Zion National Park